COAST 2 COAST 2 COAST

INDIGENOUS LIFE IN CANADA: PAST, PRESENT, FUTURE

TREATIES

BY SIMON ROSE

CONTENT CONSULTANT

AGNES PAWLOWSKA-MAINVILLE, PHD, ASSISTANT PROFESSOR, FIRST NATIONS STUDIES, UNIVERSITY OF NORTHERN BRITISH COLUMBIA

Coast2Coast2Coast is published by Beech Street Books
27 Stewart Rd. Collingwood, ON Canada L9Y 4M7

www.beechstreetbooks.ca

Produced by Red Line Editorial

Photographs ©: Library and Archives Canada, cover, 1, 16; NativeStock/North Wind Picture Archives, 4–5, 13; SuperStock/Glow Images, 7; North Wind Picture Archives, 8–9; Red Line Editorial, 10–11; Olaf Krüger/ImageBroker RM/Glow Images, 14–15; Nancy Carter/North Wind Picture Archives, 18–19; Marzolino/Shutterstock Images, 20; Kevin Frayer/Canadian Press/AP Images, 22–23; Keith Beaty/The Toronto Star/ZumaPress/Newscom, 25; Chris Cheadle/All Canada Photos/Glow Images, 26–27; Andy Clark/Reuters/Newscom, 29

Editor: Marie Pearson
Designer: Nikki Farinella

Library and Archives Canada Cataloguing in Publication

Rose, Simon, 1961-, author
        Treaties / by Simon Rose.

(Indigenous life in Canada : past, present, future)
Includes bibliographical references and index.
Issued in print and electronic formats.
ISBN 978-1-77308-123-6 (hardcover).--ISBN 978-1-77308-183-0 (softcover).--
ISBN 978-1-77308-243-1 (PDF).--ISBN 978-1-77308-282-0 (HTML)

        1. Native peoples--Canada--Government relations--Juvenile literature.
2. Native peoples--Canada--Treaties--Juvenile literature. 3. Native peoples--
Land tenure--Canada--Juvenile literature. 4. Native peoples--Legal status,
laws, etc.--Canada--Juvenile literature. I. Title.
E92.R664 2017   j323.1197071   C2017-903027-2
                                                    C2017-903028-0

Printed in the United States of America
Mankato, MN
August 2017

TABLE OF CONTENTS

CHAPTER ONE
Living Together in Peace and War 4

CHAPTER TWO
Why There Are Treaties 8

CHAPTER THREE
Treaty Rights and Obligations 14

CHAPTER FOUR
Different Views 18

CHAPTER FIVE
Modern Treaties 22

CHAPTER SIX
The Future 26

Glossary 30
To Learn More 31
Index 32
About the Author 32

LIVING TOGETHER IN PEACE AND WAR

Indigenous Peoples lived in modern-day Canada long before Europeans arrived in the early 1500s. Indigenous Peoples helped early European settlers survive the cold winters. Nations such as the Algonquin, Iroquois, and Mi'kmaq also traded with the settlers for furs and food supplies.

Gradually more settlers came to Canada. Indigenous Peoples and settlers had conflicts about who had rightful use of the local land and its resources. So they made

Indigenous Peoples including the Cree traded with Europeans for items such as knives and twine.

treaties to settle the disputes. A treaty is an agreement between two or more rulers or nations. Treaties can be made for trade, to set up wartime **alliances**, or to make peace after a conflict.

Indigenous Treaties

Making treaties was not new to Indigenous Peoples. Indigenous nations made treaties with each other long before the Europeans arrived. These agreements identified nations' territories and

THE GREAT LAW OF PEACE OF THE PEOPLE OF THE LONGHOUSE

The Great Law of Peace of the People of the **Longhouse** is one of the oldest treaties in Canada. It was a treaty of the six nations known as the Iroquois Confederacy. The Great Law dates from before 1450. The treaty has 117 **terms** about relationships between the nations, their laws, and their customs.

laws. Agreements also made sure that each nation understood the different customs of the others. Many of these agreements were not written down, and most were recorded **orally**. Others were written on birch bark

Wampum belts used pictures to remind a reciter what comes next.

or woven into wampum belts. Everyone knew what each side had agreed to.

Indigenous nations' customs were also recorded orally. Indigenous Peoples and Europeans had different views about land ownership. To Indigenous Peoples, no one could own the land. Land was for everyone to share, as were its resources. It would be passed on to their children. So the European view on land—that it could be owned or given to someone else—was a new concept for Indigenous Peoples. It was also very different from their core beliefs.

CHAPTER TWO

WHY THERE ARE TREATIES

Treaties were the way Europeans tried to settle conflicts. They used treaties to form agreements with Indigenous Peoples. But many treaties sparked conflict.

In the 1700s Britain and France both made treaties with Indigenous Peoples in an attempt to gain control of North America. In 1701 the Great Peace treaty ended almost 100 years of fighting between New France and the Iroquois Confederacy. This helped trade between the Iroquois and French run smoothly. But it also paved the way for European settlement farther west.

The nations of the Iroquois Confederacy lived by Lake Ontario in the early 1700s.

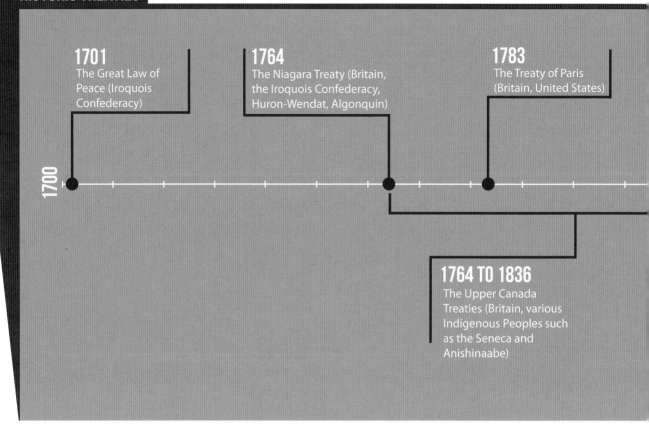

1700

1701
The Great Law of Peace (Iroquois Confederacy)

1764
The Niagara Treaty (Britain, the Iroquois Confederacy, Huron-Wendat, Algonquin)

1783
The Treaty of Paris (Britain, United States)

1764 TO 1836
The Upper Canada Treaties (Britain, various Indigenous Peoples such as the Seneca and Anishinaabe)

The British gained control of New France from the French in 1763, at the end of the Seven Years' War (1756–1763). The British government signed treaties with Indigenous nations to acquire land that Indigenous Peoples traditionally occupied. Settlers would live on this land and develop it. Indigenous nations believed they were agreeing to share their land and its resources with the newcomers, but Europeans believed Indigenous Peoples were surrendering their interests.

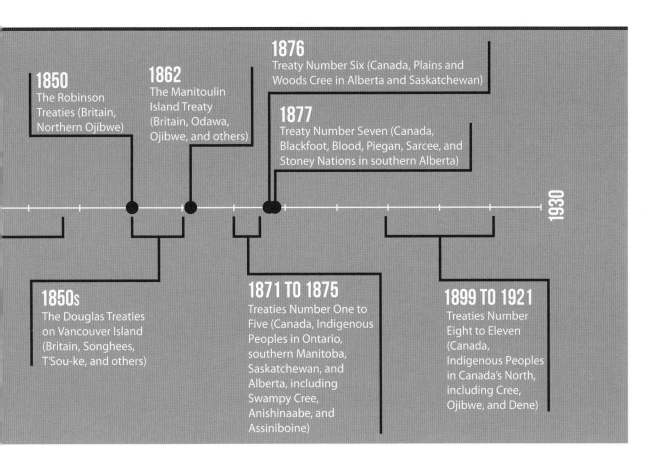

1850
The Robinson Treaties (Britain, Northern Ojibwe)

1862
The Manitoulin Island Treaty (Britain, Odawa, Ojibwe, and others)

1876
Treaty Number Six (Canada, Plains and Woods Cree in Alberta and Saskatchewan)

1877
Treaty Number Seven (Canada, Blackfoot, Blood, Piegan, Sarcee, and Stoney Nations in southern Alberta)

1930

1850s
The Douglas Treaties on Vancouver Island (Britain, Songhees, T'Sou-ke, and others)

1871 TO 1875
Treaties Number One to Five (Canada, Indigenous Peoples in Ontario, southern Manitoba, Saskatchewan, and Alberta, including Swampy Cree, Anishinaabe, and Assiniboine)

1899 TO 1921
Treaties Number Eight to Eleven (Canada, Indigenous Peoples in Canada's North, including Cree, Ojibwe, and Dene)

The government took away Indigenous Peoples' rights but said they could still hunt and fish on the land. In many treaties, the government also gave money and gifts to Indigenous Peoples as a promise of this peaceful relationship and in exchange for their land rights. This treatment of Indigenous Peoples was unfair as it never fully compensated them for trying to take their rights away.

The Government of Canada

In 1867 Canada became a country through the British North America Act. The new Canadian government quickly made treaties in the West. These treaties opened up more land for Europeans to settle.

Indigenous nations signed these treaties for many reasons. Some in western Canada, such as the Blackfoot, wanted to avoid the types of wars that had taken place in the American West. Others made treaties in order to survive. Indigenous Peoples were suffering from diseases the Europeans had introduced. They were also starving. Europeans had overhunted bison and other large animals that many nations relied on for food. The government agreed to protect Indigenous rights to hunt and fish, and it provided farming equipment to some groups.

At first the government did not sign many treaties with Indigenous Peoples in the North. There were few settlers there. But when gold was discovered in Yukon in 1896, settlers began mining minerals. So the Canadian

Hunting was an important part of traditional Cree life in the 1800s, as it provided them with food and clothing.

government signed treaties with the northern Indigenous Peoples. In 1899 they signed Treaty Number Eight with nations including the Cree. Indigenous nations agreed to sign the treaties only as long as nothing would change their way of life. They agreed—some unwillingly—to surrender land for mining and lumber operations. In return the government would protect their traditional hunting, fishing, and trapping activities there. To this day, the government pays members of these nations $5 per year.

CHAPTER THREE

TREATY RIGHTS AND OBLIGATIONS

Treaties came with certain rights and obligations for each party involved. The Upper Canada Land Surrender Treaties (1764–1862) gave First Nations money, one-time payments, and gifts, as well as created **reserves** in exchange for land for new European settlements and roads. Many First Nations now prefer the term First Nation community and no longer use reserve. The Robinson Treaties of 1850 allowed the Canadian government to mine minerals on the shores of Lakes Huron and Superior.

In 2011, 360,620 people lived on reserves, such as the Gitga'at village in Hartley Bay, British Columbia.

This historic map shows the areas affected by the Robinson-Superior and Robinson-Huron Treaties. How does this map show you how the lives of Indigenous Peoples were changed by the treaty?

The Northern Ojibwe, who occupied much of these lands, received money and were sent to reserves that were not occupied by non-Indigenous people. Their right to hunt and fish on the lands given to the government was protected.

But treaties were often not equal exchanges. The Numbered Treaties gave Canada land in northwestern Ontario, southern Manitoba, Saskatchewan, Alberta, and a large part of the Northwest Territories. In return Indigenous nations were given clothes and small sums of money. The government promised to build schools on reserves. The government did not keep many of the promises made in the treaties.

Some Indigenous groups, such as the Cree, tried to resist giving up their land to settlers in **negotiations** for Treaty Six. Money and reserves did little to make up for the resources their land provided. There were very few bison left in the area by this time. Indigenous Peoples were starving and suffered from European diseases. They felt they had to sign treaties with the government simply to survive.

THE INDIAN ACT

The government wanted to control Indigenous nations, so the Canadian government passed the Indian Act in 1876. The word "Indian" was often used to refer to Indigenous Peoples. The Act banned some very important traditions, cultural practices, and religious ceremonies of many First Nations. First Nations had no say about the terms in the Indian Act, and many disliked it. Parts of the Act were later removed, but the Indian Act still governs the relationship between the Canadian government and Indigenous Peoples in Canada.

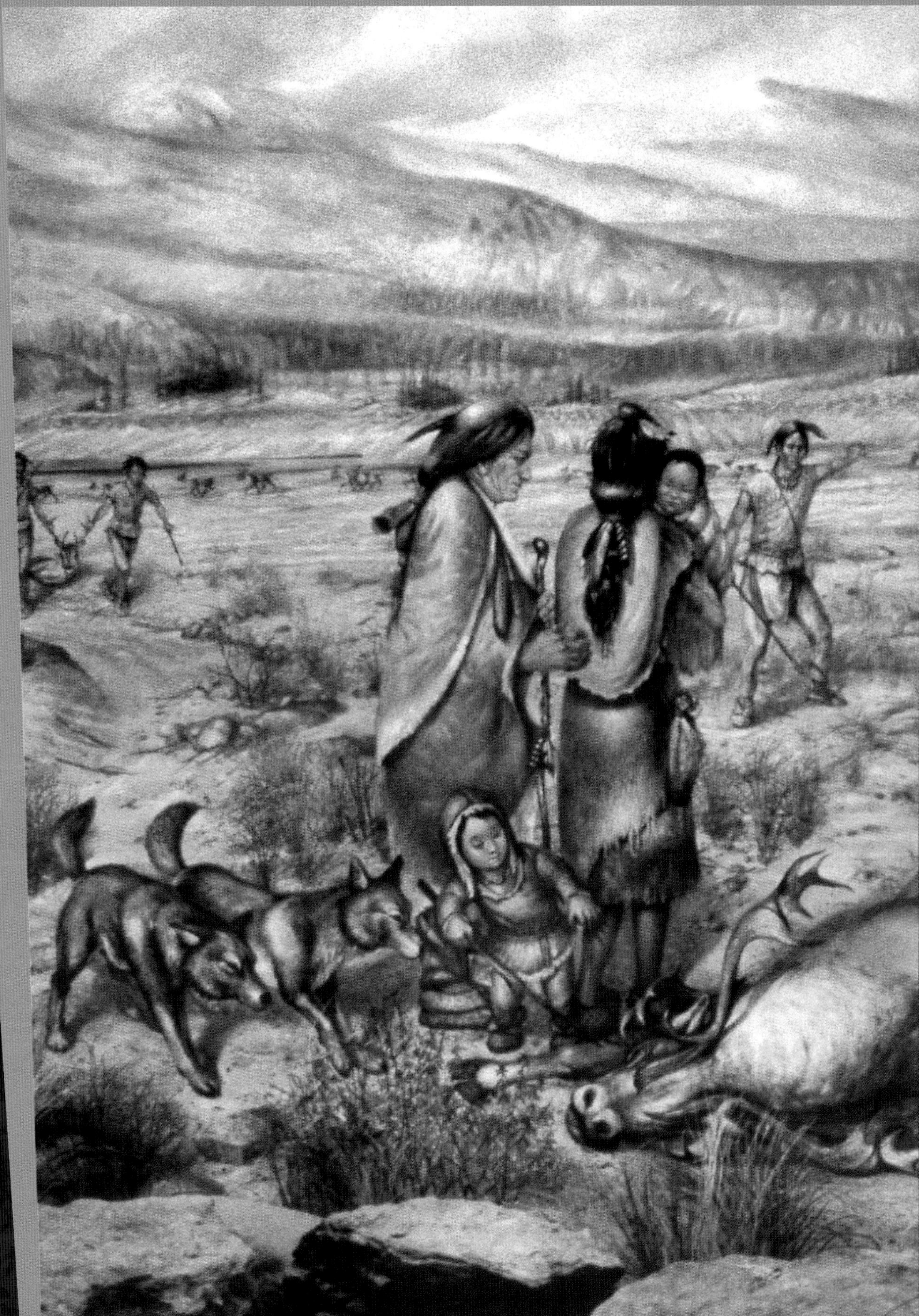

CHAPTER FOUR

DIFFERENT VIEWS

E uropean settlers and Indigenous Peoples had different views about the treaties that they had signed. From the Canadian government's perspective, treaties made it official that Indigenous nations had given up their land forever. Indigenous People were forced to live on small reserves. The government saw the $5 payments offered each year to Indigenous Peoples as payments for the land.

The government forced Indigenous Peoples to give up large areas of valuable land and to learn the European way of life. The government also wanted Indigenous Peoples to forget their cultures, languages, and religions.

The Canadian government wanted Indigenous Peoples to rely on farming for food and abandon their hunting practices.

Some Saulteaux Ojibwe people fished at night by torchlight.

They expected Indigenous Peoples to become part of Canadian society. This affected many Indigenous nations. For example, many of the Numbered Treaties included sections about providing agricultural help to First Nations such as the Saulteaux Ojibwe. There was an underlying meaning. The government was trying to persuade the Saulteaux to become more European.

When Indigenous nations signed treaties, they did so as independent nations. The treaties set up the relationship between their nations and the new Canadian government.

FRAMING QUESTIONS

Why are the Canadian government's treaties with Indigenous Peoples not fair? Could there have been another way for Indigenous Peoples and settlers to share the land?

The government told Indigenous Peoples that they would help them adjust to the changing life in North America. When signing the treaties, Indigenous nations thought the settlers only wanted to farm some of the land. They did not believe they were giving up their land for good. They also never planned to give up their cultures. From 1885 to 1951, the government banned important cultural ceremonies such as the Sun Dance. Nations including the Blackfoot and Sarcee were not allowed to practise this traditional ceremony.

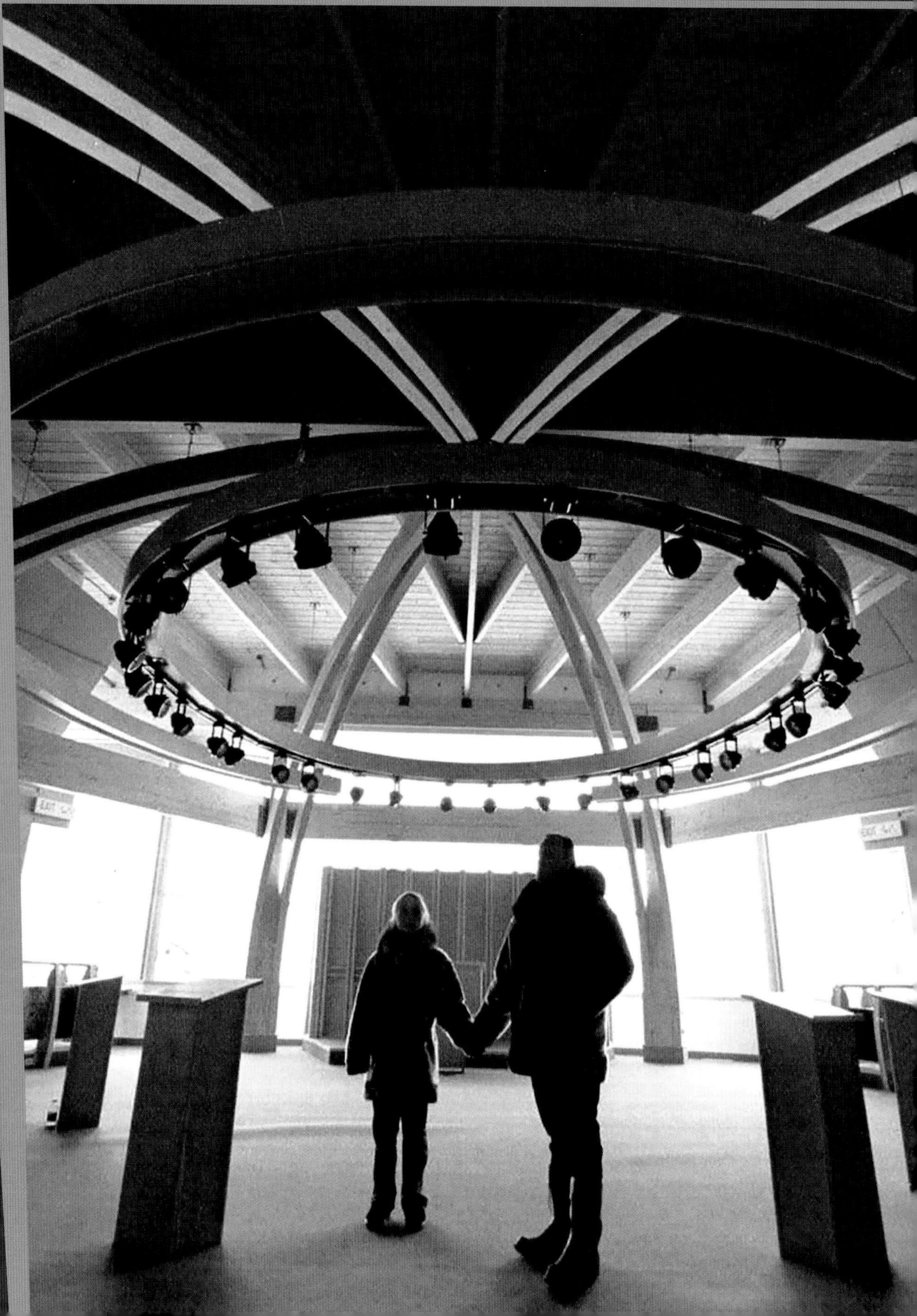

CHAPTER FIVE

MODERN TREATIES

Most of the treaties between the Canadian government and Indigenous Peoples were signed long ago. However, treaties have also been made in recent history. Relations between the Canadian government and Indigenous Peoples have often been tense. In 1992 the Charlottetown Accord tried to change the Canadian Constitution to recognize Indigenous self-governance. This would have given much more freedom to many Indigenous nations, as currently Indigenous Peoples must make treaties to self-govern.

Some Indigenous Peoples have gained the right to self-government through land claims. Inuit in Nunavut make laws in the Nunavut legislative building.

However, the Accord did not get enough votes across Canada in a national **referendum**.

Indigenous people have had to fight to keep their cultures, rights, and languages. Some of the recent modern treaties try to ease these tensions. Land claims are one of the most common modern treaties. Land claims are often made with nations that have not carried out treaties with the Canadian government in the past. Land claims may also be made when the government has misused Indigenous Peoples' resources or neglected promises made in the treaties from long ago.

CELEBRATING SUCCESS: CREATING A TERRITORY

The Nunavut Land Claims Agreement Act of 1993 was a land-rights treaty between the Government of Canada, the Government of the Northwest Territories, and the Tunngavik Federation of Nunavut. This was the first modern treaty in British Columbia. It led to the creation of the Nunavut Territory in the eastern Arctic six years later. It represents nearly 22 percent of the area of Canada.

The Mississaugas of the New Credit First Nation settled a land claim with the Government of Canada in 2010.

In 1998 the Government of Canada signed a land-claims treaty with the Nisga'a nation. The nation received almost $200 million over 15 years and control of **natural resources**. But what they received was only 5 percent of their traditional land.

Land claims are still being negotiated today. In 2016 the Algonquins of Ontario signed an Agreement-in-Principle with the Governments of Ontario and Canada, the first step to signing a treaty to settle a large land claim covering 36,000 square kilometres in Ontario.

CHAPTER SIX

THE FUTURE

There are still issues that need to be resolved in future treaties. These include developing land and paying **royalties** to Indigenous owners. Future land claim agreements might cover a variety of other issues, too. These may include protecting the environment, fish, wildlife, and national parks. Indigenous nations and both the federal and provincial or territorial governments will discuss settling many issues with Indigenous groups, mostly through payments. This money would help improve the well-being of Indigenous Peoples. Canada has also become involved in international efforts to improve the lives of Indigenous Peoples. In 2007 the United Nations, an organization created to keep order

Self-government helps Indigenous Peoples take care of their lands. The Nisga'a use fish wheels to monitor the number of salmon returning to the Nass River.

around the world, adopted the Declaration on the Rights of Indigenous Peoples. This describes the rights of Indigenous Peoples all over the world. These rights include the right to form communities, receive education and health care, and maintain culture, language, and religion. The Declaration bans discrimination against Indigenous people. It protects their right to remain distinct from the mainstream society in their country. But it has little power. Countries that adopt it are not required to follow it.

At first, Canada, Australia, New Zealand, and the United States voted against the Declaration. These countries believed that the level of self-government mentioned in the Declaration would take away the authority of their own governments. They would have less power over land claims and natural resource ownership. But in 2016, following pressure from Indigenous and human rights organizations, the Canadian government became a full supporter. Still, the government does not consider the

Indigenous groups including the Assembly of First Nations worked to persuade the Canadian government to support the Declaration on the Rights of Indigenous Peoples.

Declaration to be part of Canadian law. The government promises in the future to form partnerships and work with Indigenous Peoples of Canada based on the terms of the Declaration. Many people are hopeful that this will lead to reconciliation between Indigenous Peoples and non-Indigenous people.

GLOSSARY

ALLIANCES

unions where two or more nations agree to work together

LONGHOUSE

a communal dwelling used by some Indigenous Peoples, including the Iroquois and Huron-Wendat

NATURAL RESOURCES

things such as land, forests, water, and mineral deposits

NEGOTIATIONS

two or more sides working together to come to an agreement

ORALLY

spoken out loud

REFERENDUM

a proposed law put to popular vote

RESERVES

areas of land set apart by the federal government for the use and benefit of Indigenous Peoples and where Indigenous Peoples can choose to live

ROYALTIES

money paid to the owner of a property for the right to use it

TERMS

conditions that define the scope of a law or an agreement

TO LEARN MORE

BOOKS

Corrigan, Kathleen. *First Nations and Early Explorers*. North Mankato, MN: Capstone, 2016.

Lunn, Janet, and Christopher Moore. *The Story of Canada*. Toronto, Ontario: Scholastic Canada, 2016.

Silvey, Diane. *The Kids Book of Aboriginal Peoples in Canada*. Toronto, Ontario: Kids Can Press, 2012.

WEBSITES

Canada: A Country by Consent—Seven Treaties Signed 1871–1877
http://www.canadahistoryproject.ca/1871-97/1871-03-seven-treaties.html

Canada: Agreements under Negotiation
https://www.aadnc-aandc.gc.ca/eng/1100100031846/1100100031847

The Canadian Encyclopedia—Indigenous Peoples: Treaties
http://www.thecanadianencyclopedia.ca/en/article/aboriginal-treaties

First Nations in Canada
https://www.aadnc-aandc.gc.ca/eng/1307460755710/1307460872523

INDEX

Algonquins, 5, 10, 25

Blackfoot, 11, 12, 21
British North America Act, 11

Canadian government, 11–13,
   15–17, 19–21, 23–25, 27–29
Charlottetown Accord, 23
Cree, 11, 12, 17
cultures, 17, 20, 21, 24, 28

Declaration on the Rights of
   Indigenous Peoples, 28–29

environment, 27
Europeans, 5–7, 9–12, 15, 17,
   19, 20

fishing, 11, 12, 13, 16

Great Law of Peace of the
   People of the Longhouse,
   6, 10

hunting, 11, 12, 13, 16

Indian Act of 1876, 17
Iroquois Confederacy, 5, 6, 9, 10

Nisga'as, 25
Northern Ojibwe, 11, 16
Numbered Treaties, 11, 12,
   16, 20
Nunavut Land Claims
   Agreement Act of 1993, 24

reserves, 15–17, 19
Robinson Treaties of 1850, 11, 15

Saulteaux Ojibwe, 20
self-governance, 23, 27, 28

Upper Canada Land Surrender
   Treaties, 10, 15

ABOUT THE AUTHOR

Simon Rose is a Calgary author of 10 novels and more than
80 non-fiction books. Simon offers programs for schools, online
workshops, and courses and is an instructor for adults with the
University of Calgary and Mount Royal University. Simon also works
as an editor, a writing coach, and a copywriter.